Carving Wooden
Finger Puppets *and* Cane Toppers

20 WHIMSICAL PROJECTS FROM BASSWOOD EGGS

Ross Oar

FOX CHAPEL
PUBLISHING

Dedication

I would like to dedicate this book to Morgan and Spencer Arts, my grandchildren.

About the Author

Ross Oar began carving at the age of 10. He majored in art, and continued practicing the skill of carving while in the Navy to pass the long days at sea. Further experiences with graphic arts, metalworking, and carving have cemented art as a central part of Ross's everyday life. Ross lives in West Falls, New York, with his wife, Barb. Ross is also the author of *Carving Wooden Santas, Elves & Gnomes*.

© 2008 by Fox Chapel Publishing Company, Inc.

Carving Wooden Finger Puppets and Cane Toppers is an original work, first published in 2008 by Fox Chapel Publishing Company, Inc. The patterns contained herein are copyrighted by the author. Readers may make copies of these patterns for personal use. The patterns themselves, however, are not to be duplicated for resale or distribution under any circumstances. Any such copying is a violation of copyright law.

ISBN 978-1-56523-389-8

Publisher's Cataloging-in-Publication Data

Oar, Ross.

    Carving wooden finger puppets and cane toppers : 20 whimsical projects from basswood eggs / Ross Oar. -- 1st ed. -- East Petersburg, PA : Fox Chapel Publishing, c2008.

        p. ; cm.

      ISBN: 978-1-56523-389-8

      1. Wood-carving--Patterns. 2. Finger puppets. 3. Staffs (Sticks, canes, etc.)--Patterns. 4. Eggs in art. I. Title.

TT199.7 .O37 2008   2008033988
736/.4--dc22   2008

To learn more about the other great books from Fox Chapel Publishing, or to find a retailer near you, call toll free 800-457-9112 or visit us at *www.FoxChapelPublishing.com*.

Note to Authors: We are always looking for talented authors to write new books in our area of woodworking, design, and related crafts. Please send a brief letter describing your idea to Acquisition Editor, 1970 Broad Street, East Petersburg, PA 17520.

Printed in China

First printing: November 2008

Contents

Introduction

Whether you are a beginner or at a more advanced level, carving a basswood egg is a quick and fun project to fill an afternoon. The manageable size of the basswood egg makes for an unintimidating project, and the smooth basswood grain makes carving a breeze. Furthermore, if you're looking to get a glimpse of what the world of basswood egg carving can offer, look no farther—this book covers a variety of unusual and interesting egg-carving ideas, from finger puppets to relief-carved landscapes to cane toppers.

The fun animal finger puppets in the following pages will delight children of any age. After you follow the two step-by-steps—Tom Cat and Fred Frog—you will be able to create 12 more fantastic animal puppets, including Squeaker Squirrel, Chipper Chimp, and Allie Alligator. Also included are ideas for incorporating animal puppets into functional designs, like coat hangers and bottle stoppers. You can even create a house to display your finger puppets that will make them wobble and dance. Additionally, you can use any animal head as a fun cane topper. Brief instructions and a gallery of cane toppers are included to spark your imagination.

Tom Cat Step-by-Step,
page 14

Fred Frog Step-by-Step,
page 22

Allie Alligator,
page 32

Billy Parrot,
page 34

Chipper Chimp,
page 36

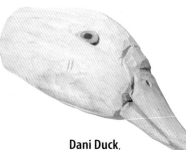

Dani Duck,
page 38

Eddie Eagle,
page 40

Fred Hound Dog,
page 42

LaToya Dachshund,
page 44

Ollie Ostrich,
page 46

Peter Panda,
page 48

Roscoe Raccoon,
page 50

Squeaker Squirrel,
page 52

Tom Tiger,
page 54

Puppet House,
page 56

Cane Toppers,
page 60

If you want to experience a different aspect of carving basswood eggs, flip to the relief-carved landscape eggs bonus section. The Covered Bridge step-by-step and five additional project ideas are included to showcase another level of basswood egg carving. These striking pieces make attractive gifts and are easy to display in your own home. Also included is a gallery of ornaments and trinkets to jump-start your imagination and get you cooking with basswood eggs!

Covered Bridge
Step-by-Step, page 64

Church,
page 74

Lighthouse,
page 74

Train,
page 75

Home Sweet Home,
page 75

River House,
page 75

Gallery,
page 76

What you need

Basswood eggs are cheaply and readily available online and in carving stores. Eggs range in size from very small to ostrich egg-sized. In this book, hen eggs (1³/₄" (4.4cm)-diameter x 2¹/₂" (6.4cm) high) and goose eggs (2¹/₄" (5.7cm)-diameter x 3³/₄" (8.3cm) high) are used. You can also make your own egg by band sawing a basswood block to the correct dimensions and carving it to an egg shape.

You'll need a selection of carving tools, including a variety of #9 gouges, a carving knife, and a V-tool. You may also find an electric drill with a Forstner bit useful for creating finger holes in the puppets.

For finishing, you'll need a few brushes, acrylic paints, water for making washes, polyurethane, and paint thinner.

Getting Started

Tools and Materials

I use a variety of carving tools to make the projects in this book, though you could get by with a few different sizes of #9 gouges, a carving knife, and a V-tool. At several places in this book, I give you an option of tools to use. Do not think that a specific tool is necessary for completing a carving just because it says so in the book—if a tool you try does the job, then it is fine. The tools listed here are just to help you get started. Other miscellaneous materials you will need to make the projects in this book include: medium and fine sharpening stones, a leather strop, acrylic paint, and brushes. I used the paint palette pictured on page 10 to create the colors on my carvings. Be sure to keep tools sharp at all times: a sharp tool makes a sharp carving.

The tools I use are high-carbon. The knives are D2 steel. Both of these materials hold an edge for a very long time. For information on ordering the knife I use, see the resources section on page 80.

I use store-bought basswood eggs to create the projects in this book. There are several sizes available. Hen eggs measure $1^3/_4$" (4.4cm) in diameter by $2^1/_2$" (6.4cm) high. I use hen eggs to make finger puppets. Goose eggs measure $2^1/_4$" (5.7cm) in diameter by $3^1/_4$" (8.3cm) high. I use goose eggs to make my relief-carved landscape eggs.

If you wish, you can band-saw a basswood blank of the correct size from a 3" x 2" x 2" (7.6cm x 5.1cm x 5.1cm) piece of basswood to make a finger puppet. Transfer the side and front patterns from the desired project to the block and cut it out using a band saw. If you own a lathe, you could also turn a basswood egg shape.

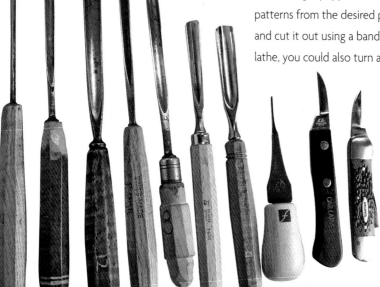

These are a few of the tools you will see me using throughout the book. From left to right: 2mm #9 gouge, 6mm #9 gouge, 10mm #9 gouge, 8mm 75° V-tool, 8mm #9 gouge, 10mm 90° V-tool, 12mm #9 gouge, micro V-tool, all-purpose carving knife, and sharp-pointed detail knife.

Carving Hints

Whether you are carving a finger puppet, a landscape, or another project out of a basswood egg, there are a few points to observe.

Safety. Carving tools are very sharp, and you must always be conscious of basic safety. Wear a Kevlar glove with rubber grip dots and don't put unnecessary pressure on the tool when your body is in the path of the cut.

Tool sharpness. Always start with sharp tools. They will make the job much easier.

Project patterns. Have a pattern or a drawing of the subject matter you wish to carve. Research your desired subject.

Pay attention to the details and make small cuts. This helps to reduce the number of mistakes. Just like making a piece of furniture, check, check, check, and THEN cut.

Start your carving by tracing the pattern on your egg. Draw on the wood in pencil before you carve a specific area. Take your time, keep your tools sharp, and check the photograph and pattern frequently to make sure you are taking off the correct areas of wood. I suggest you go through the step-by-steps first for guidance. Remember to take your time and don't become discouraged. Be brave and push the envelope toward improving your work. Woodcarving is a very rewarding hobby that you will find very relaxing. With practice, you will advance through the difficulty levels of the projects in this book and continue to improve your carving skills. Have fun!

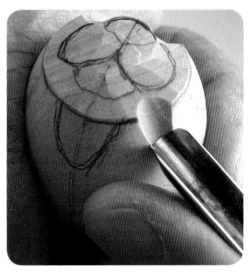

Use a pencil to sketch details and waste areas on the egg. Having this visual reference while carving really helps to keep you on the right track. Checking the pattern frequently is also a good idea.

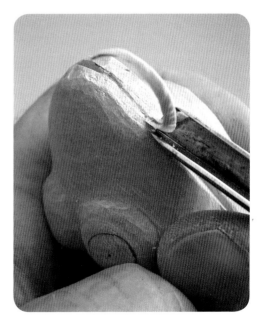

A properly sharpened tool carves smoothly through the wood and makes carving an enjoyable experience. Always start with a sharp tool—it is safer and less discouraging than hacking away with a dull edge.

Painting and Finishing Tips

When the carving is completed, wash the piece down with water. I do this with either a soft 1" (2.5cm) paint brush or a spray bottle with water. I paint when the carving is still damp because this helps to blend the paint colors and reduce any hard paint lines. I use acrylic paint washes to finish the project. I use washes because you can always go back and add a layer to darken the shade, but with undiluted paint, you are stuck with the end result. To make a wash, put a small amount of paint on your palette and start mixing water in until the color is diluted. I do not seal my carvings before I paint them. When painting, I usually cut in with a #000 brush and then fill the balance in with a #2 or #5 brush. When layering colors, add the next color before the first has dried. This way, you will create a blend of color without a hard edge between shades.

For eyes, use paint that is only slightly diluted. When the pupil is totally dry, create a highlight. I do this with a pin, fine awl, or toothpick. Dip the tip in undiluted white paint, and touch the left or right side of the eyeball. (Be sure to pick the same location in both eyes.) When the dot is dry, apply a clear gloss coating, such as Treasure Crystal Cote, which will make the eye look alive. Note that wet noses, such as a dog's, also look good with a highlight dot and a clear gloss coating.

When the carving is completely dry, apply a coat of 50-50 fast-drying polyurethane clear satin and paint thinner. This mixture seals the paint and brings out the color of the finished carving. You can use a hairdryer to dry the carving when you are finished.

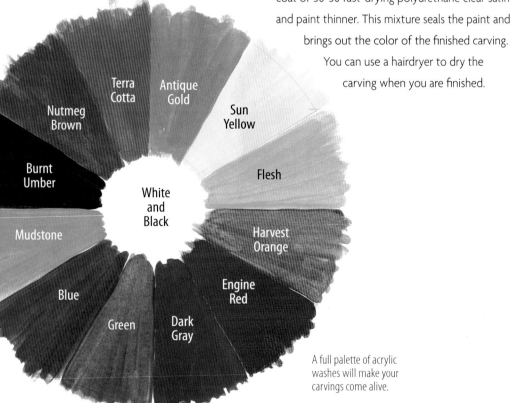

Terra Cotta
Antique Gold
Nutmeg Brown
Sun Yellow
Burnt Umber
Flesh
White and Black
Mudstone
Harvest Orange
Blue
Engine Red
Green
Dark Gray

A full palette of acrylic washes will make your carvings come alive.

1

Use a soft 1" (2.5cm) paint brush or a spray bottle to wash the animal head with water. Wetting the carving will help to blend the paint colors and avoid hard lines.

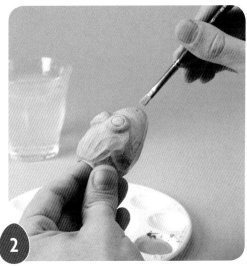

2

While the carving is still damp, apply an acrylic paint wash. Create the wash on your palette by diluting a small amount of paint with water. Use a #000 brush to cut in and a #2 or #5 brush to fill in the rest.

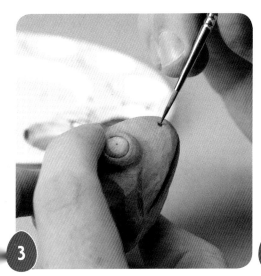

3

Paint in the details on your carving, using the photographs provided of each project as reference. Continue to use washes.

4

After painting the eye using a slightly diluted color and adding a black pupil, dip a toothpick in undiluted white and create a highlight. Study the photographs of each project to see where I apply the highlight. When the eye has dried, apply a clear gloss to make it come alive. When the carving has dried, coat it with a 50-50 mixture of fast-drying polyurethane clear satin and paint thinner.

Finger Puppets & Cane Toppers

I first started carving these animal heads as finger puppets at the woodcarving shows my wife and I attend. I would carve an animal puppet, stick it on my finger, and watch passing children's faces light up. Their reactions were always so great I began carving many different kinds of animals. Eventually, I realized all of these fun finger puppets would make a great pattern book to share with other carvers. These projects make fantastic cane toppers, too. Flip forward to page 60 to see instructions and a gallery of cane toppers. You can even use these creations to make a coat rack or bottle stopper (see "Design Ideas," page 58). If you choose to use the animal projects as finger puppets, there are several ways to wear them. Try cupping your hands and putting the puppet on the middle finger of your inside hand. Another way is to cross your arms over your chest, poke a hand out underneath your arm, and wear the puppet on one of those fingers. Whether you are carving puppets to entertain your child, grandchild, or the kid in you, I hope you enjoy creating them as much as I do!

Tom Cat
STEP-BY-STEP

Basswood hen egg

Vise

3/8" (10mm) or 1/2" (13mm) Forstner bit

Hand-held electric or battery drill

Carving knife

10mm or 12mm 90° V-tool

8mm 75° V-tool

5mm #9 gouge

8mm #9 gouge

1/4" (6mm) #9 gouge

10mm #9 gouge

12mm #5 gouge

2 blocks of 3/4" x 3/4" (19mm x 19mm) basswood

Small quick-grip clamp

Wood glue, such as Titebond #2 or Elmer's

PAINT COLORS

Yellow

Orange

Green

Pink

White

Our cover model, Kelsey Thorne, really likes Tom Cat. To create a cat finger puppet that looks like your pet, use colors of your choice. In this case, Tom Cat has a pink nose, yellow eyes with green pupils, and an orange and yellow wash on his fur.

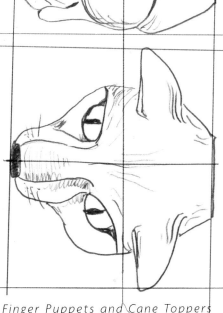

Tom Cat STEP-BY-STEP

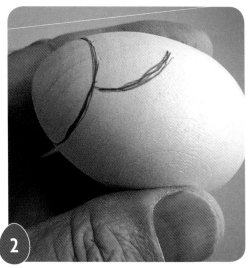

The first step is to create a finger hole in the back of the egg. Secure the egg in a vise (but don't crush it!) and drill the hole with a ⅜" (10mm) or ½" (13mm) Forstner bit. Use a bit size that most closely matches the finger size of the puppeteer or the size of the cane dowel. Be sure to bore the hole parallel with an imaginary line connecting the egg's tips. The hole should be ¾" (19mm) to 1" (2.5cm) deep. If necessary, widen the hole using a ¼" (6mm) #9 gouge.

Pencil a circle around the small end of the egg about ½" (13mm) from the tip. Draw a centerline from the tip to show the top of the head. Then, draw a line that curves from the circle to the centerline. Create a symmetrical curved line on the other side of the centerline. This curve marks an area that will be removed later.

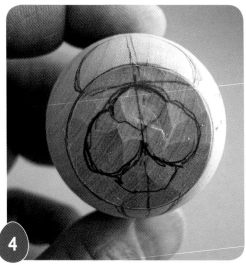

Carve the tip of the egg off with a carving knife. The surface should be a slight convex curve—not flat.

Next, draw a straight line connecting the ends of the curved lines you drew in Step 2. Use this line to mark the top of the nose. Sketch in the nose, cheeks, and mouth on the end of the egg. Be sure to center the features using the centerline.

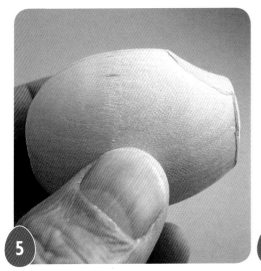

5

Use the knife to create the top of the cat's nose by carving off the semi-circle you drew in Step 2.

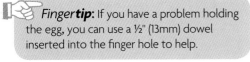

Fingertip: If you have a problem holding the egg, you can use a ½" (13mm) dowel inserted into the finger hole to help.

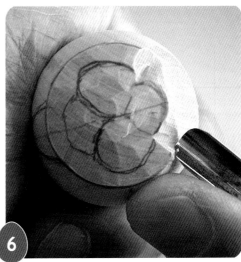

6

Use a 10mm or 12mm 90° V-tool to cut the continuation of the removed semi-circle to the pencil lines marking the intersections of the nose and cheeks. This will begin forming the edges of the nose. Next, use an 8mm #9 gouge to shape the nose.

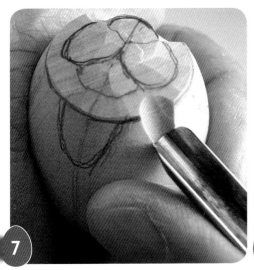

7

Use the 8mm gouge to begin shaping the snout. Make smooth cuts toward the pencil outline of the cheeks and chin.

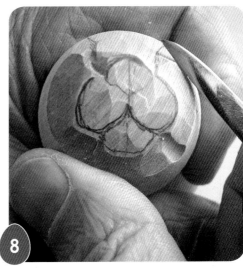

8

Draw in the bridge of the nose with a pencil. Continue shaping the face with the knife.

Tom Cat

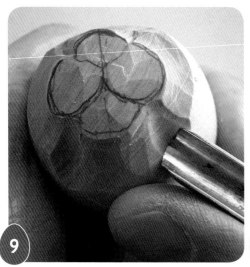

Cut out the sides of the jaw using the 8mm #9 gouge.

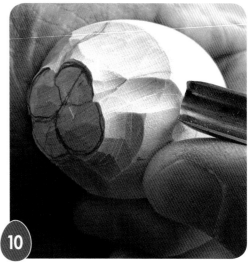

Develop the nose and eye socket areas with the 8mm #9 gouge.

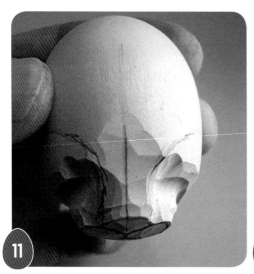

Use a 5mm #9 gouge to score cut along the sides of the nose, outlining it. Continue using the gouge to remove waste wood around the snout. With a pencil, extend the line that marks the edges of the nose and the brow bone. Also be sure to mark the centerline on the top of the head.

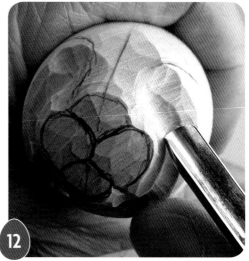

Use the 5mm #9 gouge to shape the eye socket. The eye will be nestled in the curve of the nose and brow line.

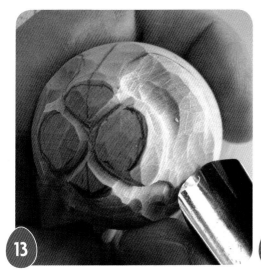

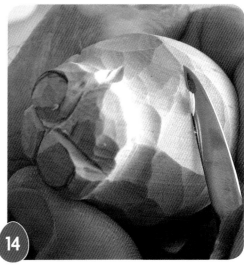

13 Use a 12mm #5 gouge to shape the sides of the head to about the halfway point on the egg. Separate the cheeks, nose, and chin. Use the knife to chip-carve along the penciled X, removing small V-shaped chips. You can also use an 8mm 75° V-tool to remove the wood from this area.

14 Use the knife to continue shaping the head. I like to have a nice slope from the back of the head into the snout. Also, shape the nose and chin by knocking off the sharp interior edges and rounding the outsides. Note that the chin is on the right in this photograph.

Fingertip: I use the 8mm 75° V-tool to shape the nose area because it has enough depth on the wings so the tool can go deep. A smaller V-tool would dig in and become stuck in the wood.

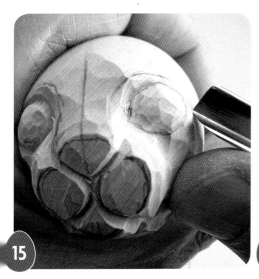

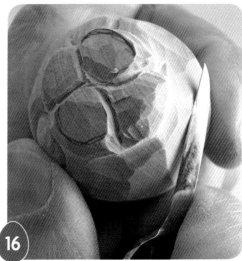

15 Pencil the large, almond-shaped eyes in. Make sure the tear duct is pointed toward the nose. Use the 8mm 75° V-tool to outline the eyeball. Then, use the knife to round the edges of the eyes so they look like the eye on the left.

16 Flatten the underside of the head using your knife.

Tom Cat STEP-BY-STEP

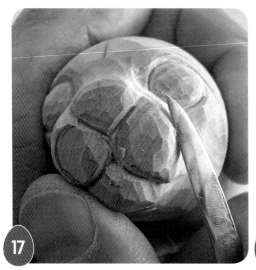

17

Shape the cheeks, making sure to knock off the sharp interior edges with your knife.

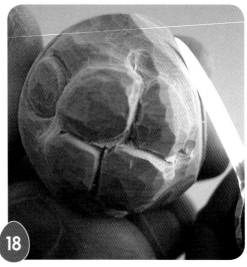

18

Form the mouth by removing the interior tip of the chin with the knife, creating a small triangular gap. Finish rounding the face.

19

When you've rounded the face, the surface should be smooth. Do a thorough inspection of the head at this point. Note the shape of the eyes—don't forget the eyelid creases. Also, remember to refine the indents at the corners of the mouth.

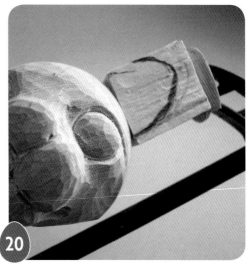

20

Cut two flat spots near the back of the head, one behind each eye. The ¾" x ¾" (19mm x 19mm) basswood blocks for the ears will be glued here. Sketch an ear shape on each block. Then, using a small quick-grip clamp to hold the ear blocks to the head one at a time, use wood glue to attach the blocks to the head.

21

After the glue has dried for 24 hours, use the knife to carve the ears out along the outline.

22

Pencil in the shape of the back of the ears, then cut them down with your knife. The shape should be thin at the top, sloping toward the back of the head.

23

Draw the lines that mark the edge of the interior of the ears. Then, use a 10mm #9 gouge to hollow out the ear. It is not necessary to hollow more than about ³/₈" (10mm) into the ear.

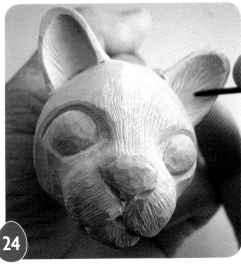

24

Next, use a micro V-tool to carve hair on the face and in the ears.

*Finger**tip***: You can try wood burning the hair on, but I find it is easier to paint the puppet when I use the micro V-tool to create the hair. Woodburning turns the carving dark brown. If I am going to paint the puppet a dark brown or black, that is fine. However, if I want to use a light color, I would need to put an extra coat of white wash on the puppet to cover up the dark lines. This extra wash can hide other details that have been carved.

Fred Frog
STEP-BY-STEP

Basswood hen egg

Vise

³⁄₈" (10mm) or ½" (13mm) Forstner bit

Hand-held electric drill

2mm #9 gouge

6mm #9 gouge

¼" (6mm) #9 gouge

8mm #9 gouge

10mm #9 gouge

Carving knife

Compass

6mm or 8mm 75° V-tool

PAINT COLORS

⚪ White   🔴 Red

🟢 Green   ⚫ Black

Yellow

This frog can be made with an open mouth or with a closed mouth. For instructions on making an open mouth, see page 29. After carving the frog smooth with a knife, wash the carving with water. Paint the skin with a blend of yellow and green. Apply a light wash of red just in the mouth opening and on the tongue. Lightly wash the belly with white. The eyes are yellow with black pupils and a clear coating on top.

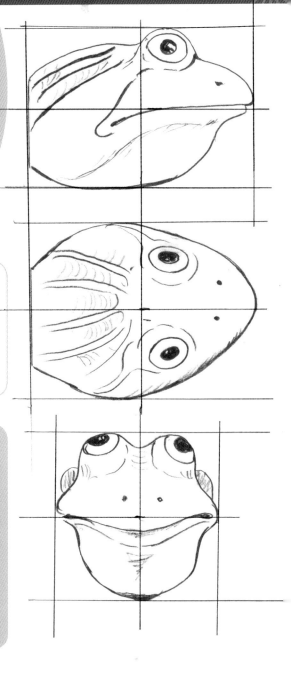

Fred Frog STEP-BY-STEP

The first step is to create a finger hole in the back of the egg. Secure the egg in a vise (but don't crush it!) and drill the hole with a ⅜" (10mm) or ½" (13mm) Forstner bit. Use a bit size that most closely matches the finger size of the puppeteer or the cane dowel. Be sure to bore the hole parallel with an imaginary line connecting the egg's tips. The hole should be ¾" (19mm) to 1" (2.5cm) deep. If necessary, widen the hole using a ¼" (6mm) #9 gouge.

Using a pencil, draw a centerline that runs through the egg tips (1). Next, draw another line that goes around the egg, also running through the tips, and intersects the first line on the tips at 90° angles (2). Draw a third line around the middle of the egg (3). Locate the position of the eyes by drawing two lines that bisect the top two quadrants of the egg lengthways (4). Where those lines and the line around the middle of the egg meet is the center of each eye (5). Draw two round eyes.

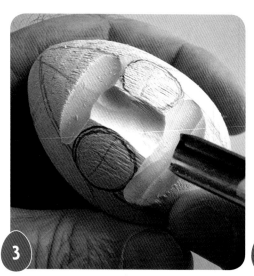

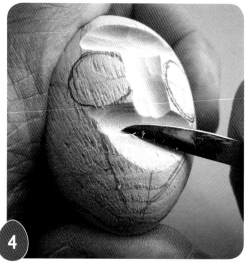

Using a 10mm #9 gouge, rough out the eyes. Create a channel across the grain on both sides of the eyes. Then, cut with the grain between the eyes. This will create an I shape around the eyes.

Next, begin removing wood from the area where the frog's nose will be. Using a carving knife, remove the wood between the two #4 lines you drew in Step 2. Cut the top of the nose to the depth of the pencil lines. The surface should be slightly curved.

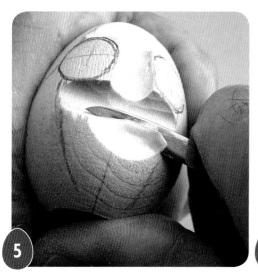

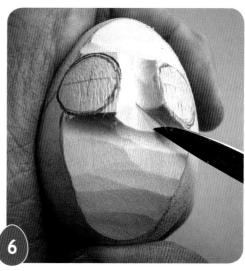

5 Turn the egg around and knife-cut the back of the head to the depth marked by the #4 pencil lines. This surface should also be slightly curved.

6 Use the knife to round the inside corners of the eyeballs.

*Finger**tip**: Be sure to look at the reference photos at the beginning of the step-by-step periodically to make sure you're on the right track.

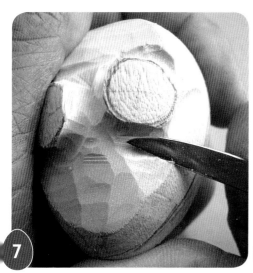

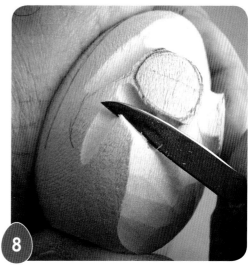

7 Cut around the eyes with the knife and an 8mm #9 gouge. Leave a small ridge on the outside of the eyes to mark the edge of the cheek areas. Note that the eyes raise up from the head.

8 Begin rounding off the head with the knife. Use the 8mm #9 gouge to delineate the cheek lines by cutting on each side, as shown.

Fred Frog

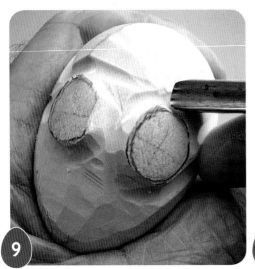

9 Continue to refine the shape of the eyes with the 8mm #9 gouge.

10 Hold the egg so the nose is pointing straight downward. Sketch a circle as shown. Then, use your knife to slice off the area within the circle. This begins the formation of the throat.

> *Finger**tip**:* Using pencil marks will help you keep your cuts more accurate when roughing out.

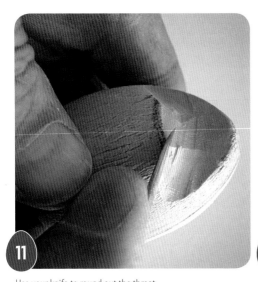

11 Use your knife to round out the throat.

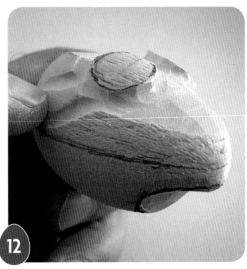

12 Stop at this point and examine your carving. Note the gouge cuts around the cheek line, the amount the eyes have been relieved, and the extent of the carving under the mouth. The egg is beginning to look like a frog!

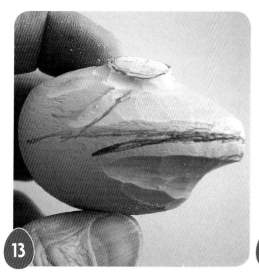

13 Draw the mouth line. Note that it dips slightly beneath line #1 at the ends. Continue to round off the throat until you've created the lower jaw back to the end of the mouth line.

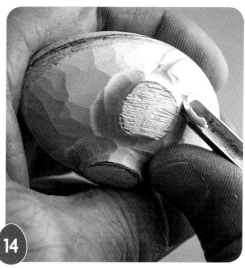

14 Return to the back of the head and continue to shape it using the 8mm #9 gouge. Continue relieving the eyes.

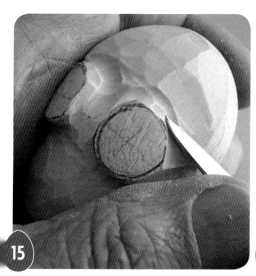

15 Begin to carve finishing cuts on the top of the head with your knife.

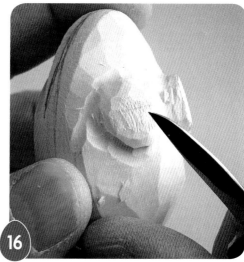

16 Still using the knife, round the eyes.

Fred Frog STEP-BY-STEP

17

After you have carved the eyes to rounded shapes, round further by making smaller cuts. This will give the eyes a finished look.

18

The basic form is now finished. Next, pencil in the eyeballs with a compass so they are circular.

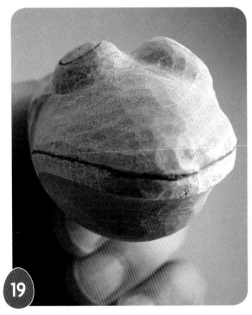

19

Check the line you've drawn for the mouth. It should follow line #1, except for where it curves down at the corners of the mouth.

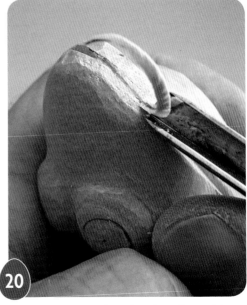

20

Using a 6mm or 8mm 75° V-tool, rough-cut the mouth line.

28   *Carving Wooden Finger Puppets and Cane Toppers*

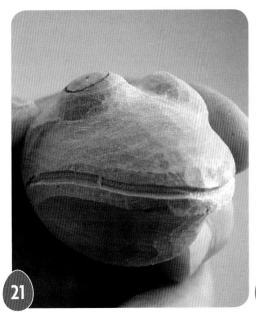

21 When you've finished V-cutting the mouth, it should look something like this.

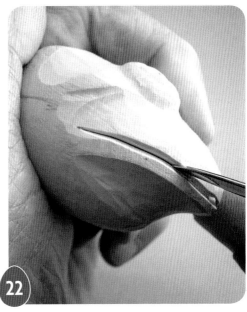

22 Cut the mouth deeper with a knife to give it more shadow.

*Finger**tip***: I carve Freddy Frog in two ways: with a line for a mouth, as demonstrated here, or with an open mouth and tongue, as pictured at the beginning of the chapter. To create a frog with an open mouth, use your knife to make a deep V into the mouth line. Clear out the excess wood. I like to use a micro V-tool to carve a groove on both the top and bottom of the inside to show where the lips end and the mouth begins. I make the U-shaped tongue from a small flat piece of basswood. It helps to shave down the back of the tongue so it will more easily wedge into the back of the mouth.

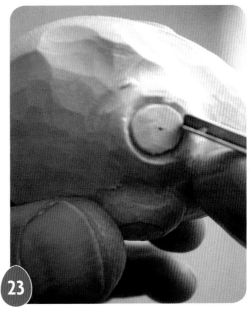

23 Use the 6mm or 8mm 75° V-tool to outline the eyeballs, following the pencil line.

Fred Frog STEP-BY-STEP

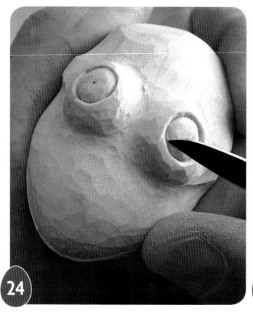

24

Using the knife, shave off the hard edges left by the 6mm or 8mm 75°V-tool so the eyeballs are round.

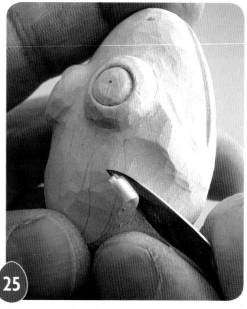

25

Carve all around the back of head and smooth out the top area. Pencil in two dots for nose holes.

26

Clean up the throat area with your knife.

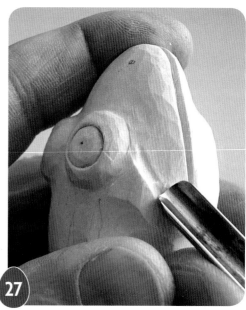

27

Use the 6mm or 8mm #9 gouge to define the front side of the cheek line.

30 *Carving Wooden Finger Puppets and Cane Toppers*

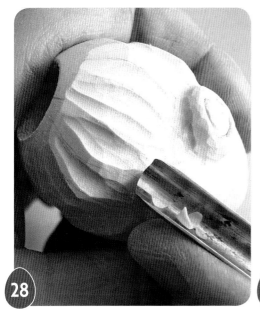

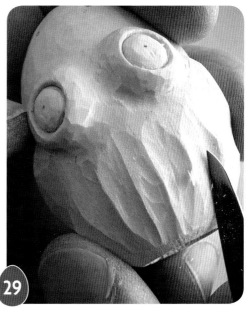

28 Use a 6mm #9 gouge to carve wrinkles in the skin at the top of the neck. I like to make five or so.

29 Clean up the wrinkles with the knife.

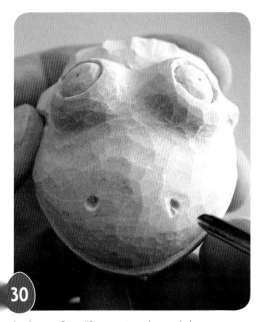

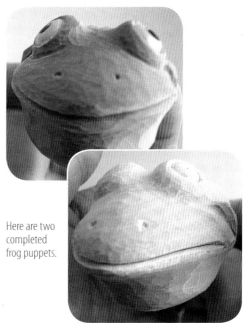

Here are two completed frog puppets.

30 Lastly, use a 2mm #9 gouge to cut the nose holes.

Allie Alligator

After you've finished carving, use a pyrography machine to burn the crosshatch and scales on the neck, the dots on the nose, and the wrinkles around the eyes and mouth. The teeth are carved from scraps of basswood and glued into the mouth. Paint the eye with burnt umber. Wash the throat, mouth, and top of the snout with a burnt umber, terra cotta, and orange blend. Paint the rest of the skin with a green and yellow mix. The teeth are painted white.

PAINT COLORS

- Green
- Yellow
- Terra Cotta
- White
- Burnt Umber
- Orange
- Black

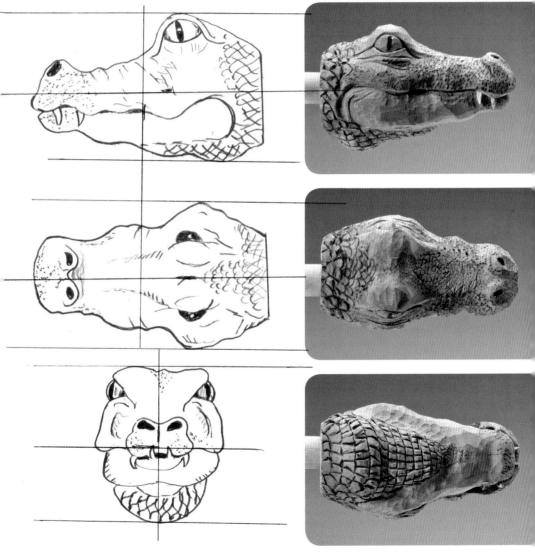

Billy Parrot

Billy Parrot is fit to perch on any scurvy pirate's shoulder. Pay special attention to the beak notch. Use a knife to carve feathers around the head or woodburn them. Paint the beak with a yellow wash, and blend red onto the tip. The beak bridge is green. Paint yellow eyes with green irises. Paint around the eyes with white and speckle with red. The top of the head is red, and the bottom is yellow and orange with green and burnt umber.

PAINT COLORS

- ● Red
- ○ White
- ◐ Yellow
- ● Black
- ● Green
- ◑ Orange
- ● Burnt Umber

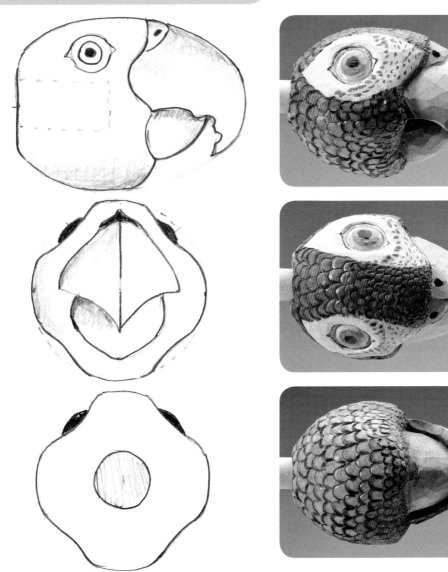

Chipper Chimp

If you like monkeying around, you'll love carving Chipper. I use a micro V-tool to carve the hair. The eyes are black. Paint the nose, mouth, ears, and eyebrows a flesh and white blend. The fur is a black and burnt umber mix.

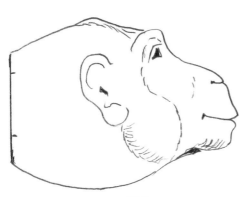
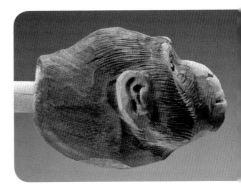

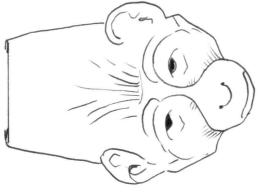

Dani Duck

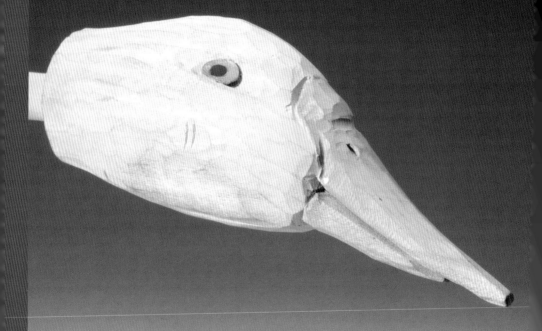

Dani can be carved from a goose egg or a basswood blank made from a block 2¼" (5.7cm) diameter x 3¼" (8.3cm) high. Paint the head with a white wash. The beak is painted with an orange and yellow mix. The eye is yellow with a black pupil.

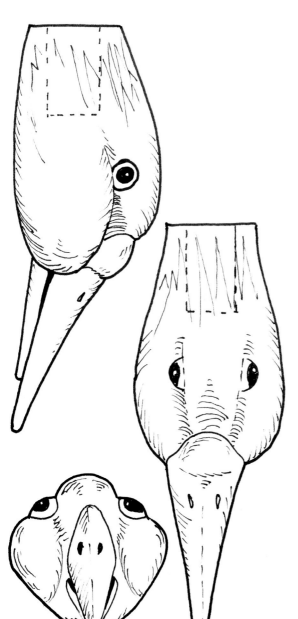

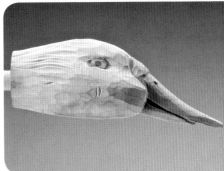

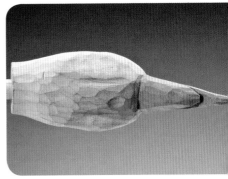

Eddie Eagle

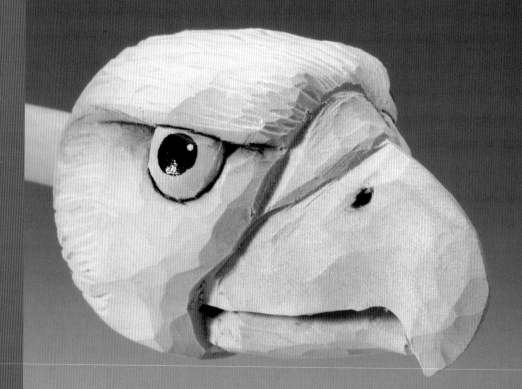

Draw a centerline on the top and side. This will help you to carve the profiles square. To carve Eddie, I use only a knife and an 8mm 75° V-tool. A ¼" (6mm) sanding stick with 120 grit is useful for maintaining roundness while sanding the eyes. To paint, apply white over the feathers and then wash with burnt umber. The beak is yellow with a burnt umber wash. The eyes are yellow with a black pupil.

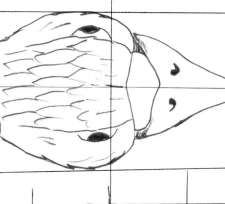

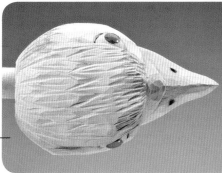

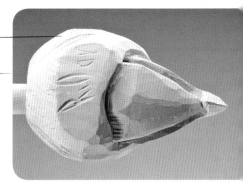

Fred Hound Dog

Children love friendly Fred. I use a knife to do the profile and the face view. I switch to a 90° V-tool to outline the ears, nose, and mouth. Paint the nose and eyes black, the mouth red, the teeth white, and use a mixture of yellow ochre and brown for the head. When dry, apply a coat of polyurethane clear satin crystal coat on the eyes.

PAINT COLORS

● Black   ● Brown

● Red   ○ White

● Yellow Ochre

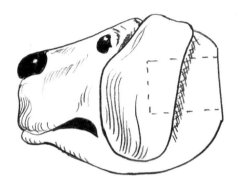

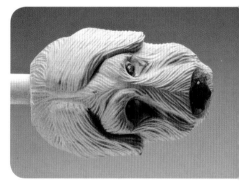

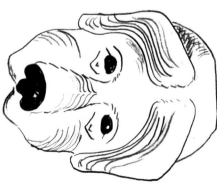

LaToya Dachshund

The name of this carving came from a visit my wife Barb and I had with Mark and Tina Akers, who have a nice dachshund. Use a micro V-tool to create the hair. The nose is wood-burned to get a nice solid black. Before painting, wash the head with water. Use washes and layer the coats each time, getting darker until the desired color is achieved. Paint the hair with a reddish brown mixed with black and burnt umber. The eyes are white with green and a black pupil. Apply a red wash in the corner of the eyes. Remember to add a white dot for reflection. Coat the nose and eyes with a clear gloss.

PAINT COLORS

- Red
- Brown
- Black
- Burnt Umber
- White
- Green

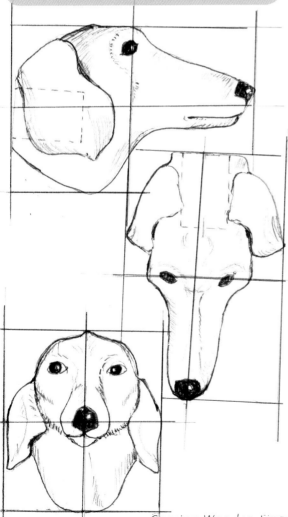

Ollie Ostrich

I enjoy comical ostriches—they are always cocking their heads and looking at you with their big eyes. Those big eyes are the trickiest part of this carving. Use a V-tool to outline the eyes, round them with a knife, and smooth them with a fine-grit sanding stick. After carving, I use a wood burner to get a nice solid black on the nose holes, throat, and eyeballs. The head is painted with white. The neck is burnt umber. The beak is a blend of red, orange, and yellow.

PAINT COLORS

○ White   ◯ Yellow

● Red   ● Burnt Umber

◐ Orange

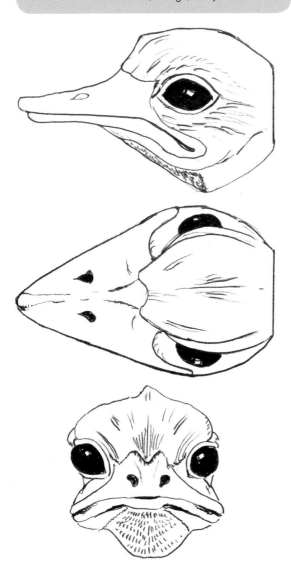

Peter Panda

I originally created Peter Panda because my wife likes pandas. After carving, use a micro V-tool to create the hair. This allows you to obtain a nice white wash. Carving the hair is the trickiest part of the panda—take your time and try to get the hairs one after the other in an organized fashion. Coat the eyes with clear gloss.

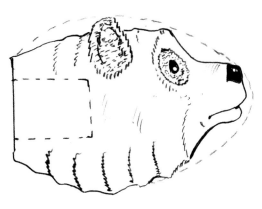

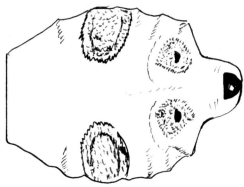

Roscoe Raccoon

You can create the raccoon from a basswood hen egg or a basswood rough-out made from a $1\frac{7}{8}$" x $2\frac{1}{2}$" (4.8cm x 6.4cm) block. Use the side and front views below to create the band saw pattern. After carving, use a wood burner on the complete head and then wash it with burnt umber. Paint the nose and eyes black, and use white on the brows, nose, and cheeks.

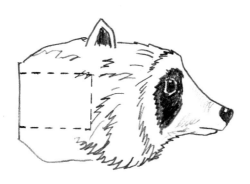

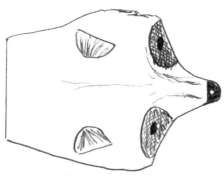

Squeaker Squirrel

After carving, use a wood burner on the whole head and the eye. Use a light burnt umber wash and light gray under the mouth, and put a white dot in the eye for reflection. When dry, apply a clear coat on the eyes to make them glossy.

PAINT COLORS

● Burnt Umber

● Light Gray

○ White

 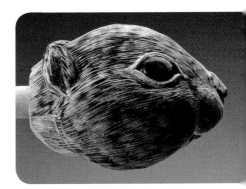

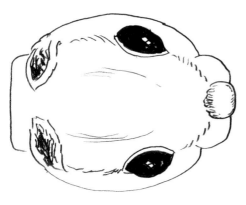 

Tom Tiger

You can glue on the ears or carve them. Use a micro V-tool to create the hair. Draw a few lines with pencil every ¼" (6mm) to help create the flow of the hair. When you've finished carving, burn the stripes. Paint the head with a blended wash of yellow and terra cotta. Paint white around the eyes and the sides of the head. The nose is pink, and the eyes are green and yellow.

PAINT COLORS

- Yellow
- Pink
- Terra Cotta
- Green
- White

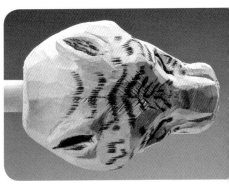

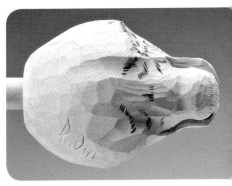

Puppet House

I created this house to put a roof over your puppets' heads. I've given the details of the house I built, but feel free to use whatever wood, size, and finish you wish. You could also create a log, or a bucket, or any other type of dwelling for your puppets. Use your imagination! The puppet can be controlled from the hidden dowel rod, or be left to wobble when the correct counter balance is used. Use a band saw to trim the wood to the correct sizes. I carved the entrance hole with my carving knife after roughing the hole with a 2" (5cm) hole saw. Finishing nails and glue were used to assemble the house. Use a micro V-tool to create the shingles on the roof. You may have to use trial-and-error to determine the correct placement of the hook and eye so the dowel will balance and wobble when a puppet is attached. Adjust the number of 1/4" (6mm) nuts as necessary. If the puppet's finger hole is too big to fit on the dowel, wrap the end of the dowel with masking tape. If the hole is too small, whittle the end of the dowel. Note: Instead of using the two blocks for the house, you might want to try stacking and gluing 3/4" (19mm)-thick pieces of wood. This will make the puppet house look as if it is made from planks.

TOOLS & MATERIALS LIST

2 blocks of 3⅜" x 3¾" x 2¼"
(8.6cm x 9.5cm x 5.7cm) basswood,
or wood of choice (house)

2 pieces of 3⅜" x 5" x ¼"
(8.6cm x 12.7cm x 6mm) basswood,
or wood of choice (roof)

1 piece of ½" (13mm)-diameter x
2⅝" (6.7cm)-long dowel rod (mount)

1¼" (3cm) metal all-thread, 1" (2.5cm) long

2 or more ¼" (6mm) nuts

Hook and eye loops

Band saw

Hole saw

Carving knife

Micro V-tool

Finishing nails

Glue

PAINT COLORS

- Red
- Brown
- Black

¼" (6mm) thread
and adjusting nuts for
counter balance

½" (13mm)-diameter dowel

Hook

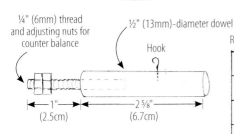

|←— 1" —→|←——— 2⅝" ———→|
(2.5cm)   (6.7cm)

Roof

¼" (6mm)-thick wood

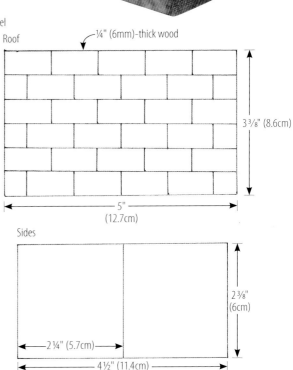

3⅜" (8.6cm)

|←———— 5" ————→|
(12.7cm)

Front and Back

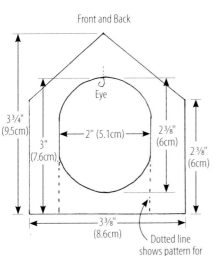

Eye

3¾"
(9.5cm)

3"
(7.6cm)

|←— 2" (5.1cm) —→|

2⅜"
(6cm)

2⅜"
(6cm)

|←——— 3⅜" ———→|
(8.6cm)

Dotted line
shows pattern for
back of house

Sides

|←— 2¼" (5.7cm) —→|

2⅜"
(6cm)

|←———— 4½" (11.4cm) ————→|

Pattern appears at 50% of actual size. Copy at 200%.

Design Ideas

Coat Hanger

To make a creative coat hanger for a child's room, carve finger puppets with holes sized to fit $\frac{1}{2}$" (13mm)-diameter dowel rods. Glue the dowels inside the puppets, and then glue the pegs into a board of your choice. Make equally spaced holes with a $\frac{1}{2}$" (13mm) Forstner bit. Let your creativity come into play—use a scroll saw to shape the board, chip carve designs or a border, or paint or carve the child's name.

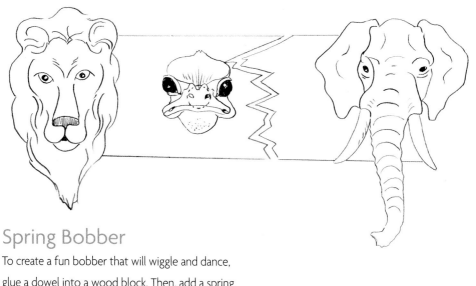

Spring Bobber

To create a fun bobber that will wiggle and dance, glue a dowel into a wood block. Then, add a spring on the dowel, and put another piece of dowel in the other end of the spring. Lastly, put the puppet head on the end of the dowel. Be sure not to make the spring too long, or the head will droop.

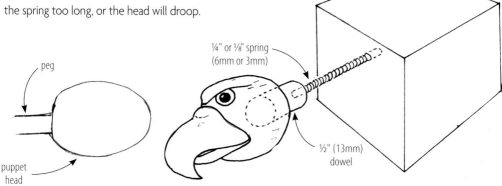

peg

puppet head

¼" or ⅛" spring (6mm or 3mm)

½" (13mm) dowel

Bottle Stoppers

Finger puppets can also be made into bottle stoppers. Buy a bottle stopper and fit the puppet on the top, or try creating your own from a piece of dowel and a cork.

puppet
head

cork

Cane Toppers

Puppet heads can be used to decorate a cane handle. Use a Forstner bit to set a dowel into the handle. Make sure the puppet hole is sized to fit the dowel, and glue it on with wood glue.

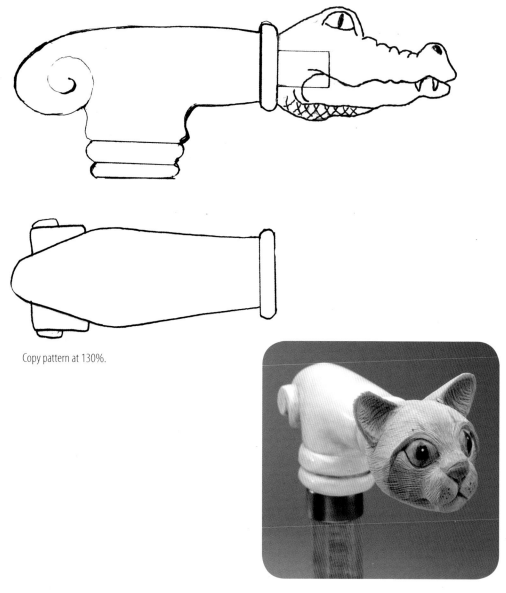

Copy pattern at 130%.

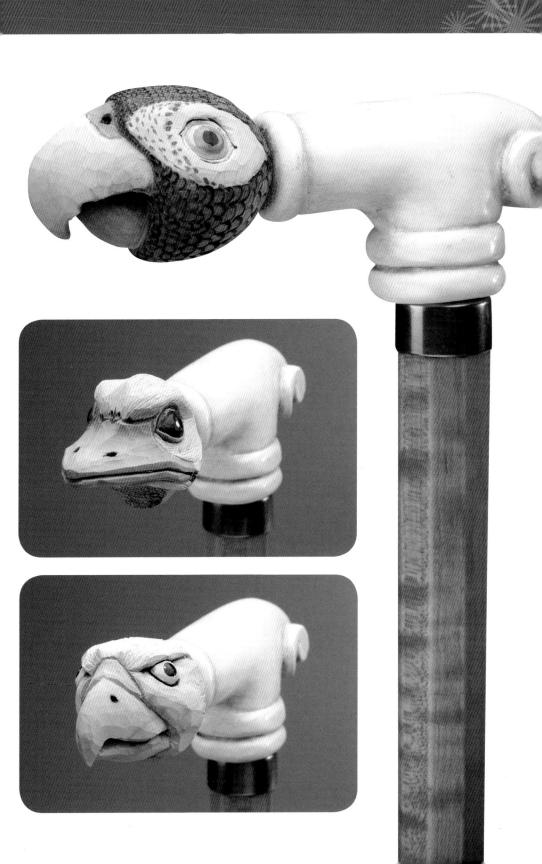

Relief-Carved Landscape Eggs

Relief-carved landscape eggs are a challenging and fun project to try after mastering finger puppets. People really seem to like them, and I always get a lot of interest in them at shows. I've included a few patterns to get you started, but the only limit is your imagination. You can carve a landscape egg that was inspired by your backyard, church, or famous or local architecture. When carving a relief landscape egg, it is important to maintain perspectives. Try to create perception of depth and to make the relief look real by using lots of shadow cuts. I use the same tools as I do to make a finger puppet with the addition of some smaller gouges. To finish the landscape eggs, I often use paint washes or three coats of polyurethane with a mix of burnt umber artist oil, linseed oil, and paint thinner on top.

Covered Bridge
STEP-BY-STEP

Basswood goose egg

Micro V-tool

¼" (6mm) 90° V-tool

10mm or 12mm 90° V-tool

Carving knife

8mm #9 gouge

Sharp pointed knife

PAINT COLORS

Green

Pink

Blue

White

This picturesque landscape features an old covered bridge spanning a creek. Pine trees tower serenely in the middle ground, while mountains dominate the background. Remember while you carve that in order for the scene to look 3-D, you must slope your carving from the front to the back. The further back an object is in the scene, the deeper it must be cut.

Covered Bridge STEP-BY-STEP

1 Using the pattern given on page 65, draw the outline of the covered bridge on the face of the egg as shown. Make sure it is drawn as a 3-D sketch.

2 Using a 10mm or 12mm 90° V-tool, cut along the pencil line about ⅛" (3mm) deep all the way around the bridge. Cut deeper at the back of the bridge. This will help you when you cut a taper to the back in Steps 3 and 4. Doing this will make the bridge appear more 3-D.

*Finger**tip***: The objective is to create an illusion of depth in the scene. When sketching patterns for relief carvings, it helps to make the shapes look 3-D. I also like to make deep cuts in the background and shallower cuts in the foreground. The combination of the relief cuts and the 3-D shapes really makes the carving pop off the surface.

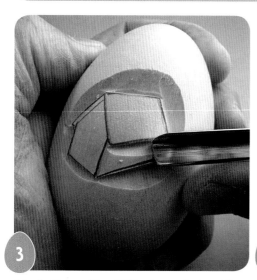

3 Using the 10mm or 12mm 90° V-tool, cut under the roof line, cutting off more in the rear of the bridge than the front. Use a sharp tool for clean cuts.

4 Next, use a carving knife to slice the wall. Remember to angle the cut so you remove a wedge with its thickest side toward the back of the egg.

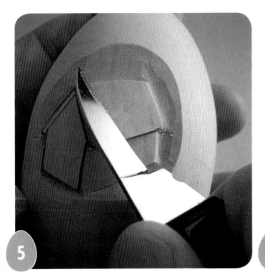

5 Using a knife, cut the plane of the roof, again tapering it to the back to create depth of field. Try to cut with the grain.

6 Stop and examine your carving. Note how the roof and side of the bridge both slope back. The wall is deeper than the roof.

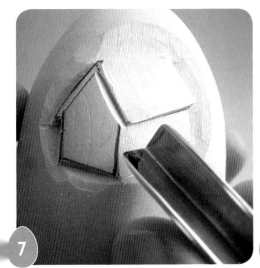

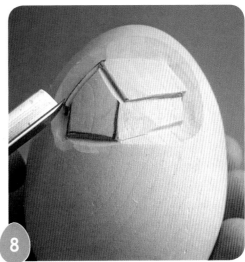

7 Using the 10mm or 12mm 90° V-tool, cut under the right side of the roof overhang on the front of the bridge. This will cause the edge of the roof to stick out.

8 Cut under the left side of the roof overhang using the 10mm or 12mm 90° V-tool.

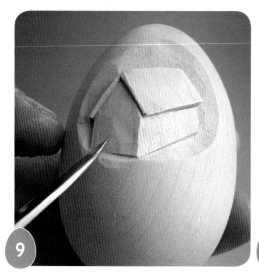

9

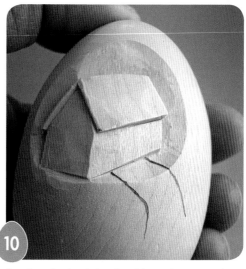

10

Knife-cut a taper on the front of the bridge, with the high point on the left edge. Make clean cuts. Also, cut the left side of the roof edge so it has a flat surface. Cut the right side of the roof edge at an angle back toward the right side of the roof. Shaping the roof edges in this way will add to the 3-D look.

Draw lines showing the location of the creek running under the bridge.

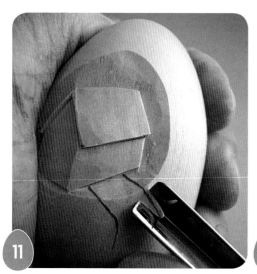

11

12

Cut out the edges of the waterway using the 10mm or 12mm 90° V-tool.

Use the knife to carve out the creek.

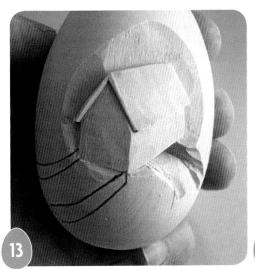

13 Sketch the road and fences on the foreground.

14 Then, using the ¼" (6mm) 90° V-tool, carve around the inside fence lines. Draw the opening onto the front of the bridge.

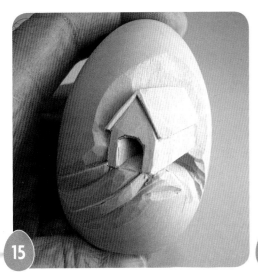

15 Use the ¼" (6mm) 90° V-tool to cut the outside of the fence lines. Next, use the knife to carve down the road and around the outside of the fences. Also, use the knife to remove the waste wood in the bridge opening.

16 Draw in trees and rough-cut them with a 10mm 90° V-tool.

*Finger**tip**:* Be sure your tools are razor-sharp. Stop and strop them if you haven't already. Sharp tools are key when doing relief carving and making smooth planes.

Covered Bridge STEP-BY-STEP

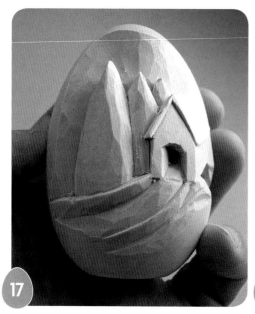

17

Cut and shape the trees, rounding them off with the knife as shown. The trees should really stand off the surface behind them, and the tips should be completely cut free of the egg.

18

Draw mountains in the background. Then, use the 10mm 90° V-tool and knife to relieve them.

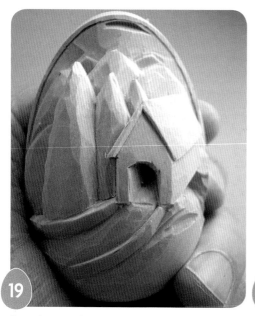

19

Draw a line around the edge of the egg face, above the mountains.

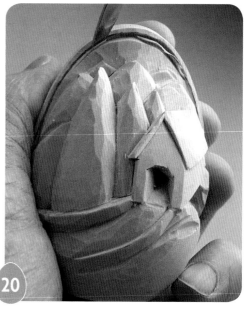

20

Using your knife, begin removing wood on the inside of the line.

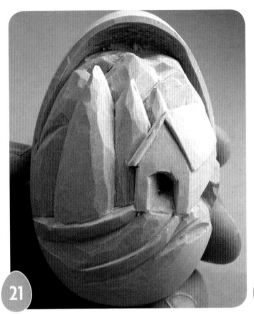

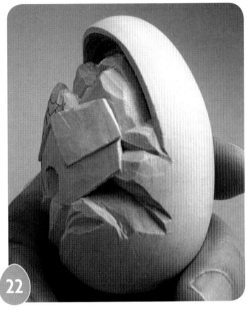

21 Switch to an 8mm #9 gouge and continuing hollowing under the line. This will create shadows in the mountains.

22 Note how much wood has been removed from the egg shape. The bridge and trees should protrude a fair amount from the back of the egg.

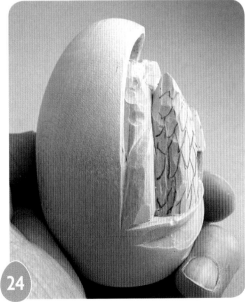

23 Use a fine pencil to draw V's to show the location of tree branches.

24 This is what the egg should look like at this point. The bridge sticks out furthest, then the trees, then the mountains, and then the egg frame.

Covered Bridge STEP-BY-STEP

25

Cut in the tree shadows using the sharp pointed knife. Make sharp triangle cuts as shown.

26

Use a micro V-tool to make fine cuts on the branches. Take your time and create texture as shown.

27

Pencil a window opening on the side of the bridge.

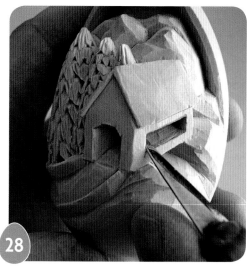

28

Using a very sharp pointed knife, cut the window opening on the bridge. The opening should slope toward an imaginary line spanning the length in the middle of the window.

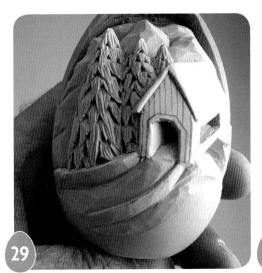

29 Draw details on the bridge. There are vertical lines to show planks, and lines around the opening and window to show support beams.

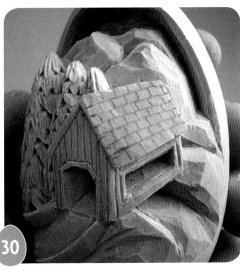

30 Cut the details using the micro V-tool. Then, pencil in shingles on the roof.

31 Cut the shingles with the micro V-tool. Draw a horizontal line to show the tops of the fences, and vertical lines for fence pickets. Use the 8mm #9 gouge to make texture lines in the road. Next, use the micro V-tool to add plank lines to the window side of the bridge.

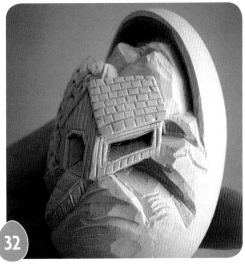

32 Finish the carving by using the micro V-tool to carve the fence lines. Switch to the 10mm or 12mm 90° V-tool to create texture cuts in the foreground.

Fingertip: There are many options for finishing your covered bridge landscape. You can leave it natural, dip it in stain, or use acrylic washes to add color. No matter what you choose, I recommend using a fingernail brush to clean the chips off.

Projects

These patterns and photographs show a few examples of what can be done with a relief-carved landscape egg. If you want to try making a landscape with a pattern of your own, sketch your desired subject, making sure there is a foreground, middle ground, and background to the piece. The middle ground is usually the focus of the piece. Be creative and don't be afraid to try your own sketches. Basswood eggs are not a costly medium to practice on, so try until you create something that pleases you.

Lighthouse

Church

Train

Home Sweet Home

River House

Gallery

Basswood eggs can be the foundation for many interesting projects. These are just a few ideas I happened to have on hand. Hopefully they will stimulate your imagination to try something new. Be creative—try making hanging ornaments, expressive faces, or even eggheads!

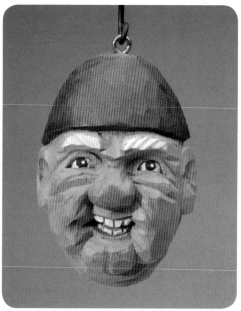

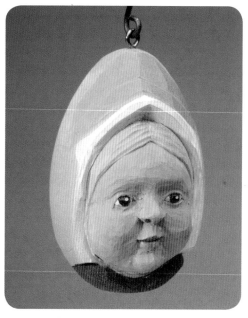